ISKCON
EDUCATIONAL
SERVICES

1 Teachers Guide
1 User-Guide
2 CD's = 1, Audio 1, CD Rom.
12 Photo cards
10 Schemes of Work
1 Reference guide

The Heart of Hinduism

9 780952 268611

AF201734

User-Guide

Instructions for Using the Resource Pack for Secondary Teachers

"The Heart of Hinduism"
A Resource Pack for Secondary Teachers
User Guide

Published by ISKCON Educational Services
Bhaktivedanta Manor, Hilfield Lane, Aldenham,
Herts. WD25 8EZ, England, UK
Tel/fax: +44 (0)1923-859578
e-mail: ies@pamho.net
website: http://www.iskcon.org.uk/ies

Cover Design by Ajay Kumar
Typesetting by Bhawesh Shah
Printed and bound by A.G. Printing & Publishing Ltd.

Not to be sold separately from "The Heart of Hinduism" Teaching Pack, which includes:

1. Teachers' Book/Reference Manual
2. CD-Rom (Information and Resources)
3. Audio CD
4. Deity Photo-cards
5. Schemes of Work
6. User Guide

Erratum

The CD-ROM now contains selected verses from the Bhagavad Gita, and not the entire book (as written on the sleeve of some versions of the CD).

Teacher Support Services:

The publishers offer all customers a free support service. If you have any queries regarding your use of your materials, or on Hinduism and its teaching within schools, then please contact ISKCON Educational Services, at the above address or as follows:
tel – 01923 859578 or 01865 304309; e-mail – ies@pamho.net
IES also offers opportunities for INSET, guest speakers and temple visits.

Contents

Index

Introduction

Congratulations on your purchase of 'The Heart of Hinduism' Teaching Pack. This publication has been designed to equip RE teachers with all the material they need in helping students learn about and learn from the Hindu tradition. In here you will find accurate and well-categorised information, over fifty related stories, photo-cards, teaching ideas, scriptural texts, audio clips, charts and pictures for classroom projection, an audio pronunciation guide – and much more. For a quick reference to all these features, please consult the index on page 3 and, for those items on the CD-ROM, the table on page 16.

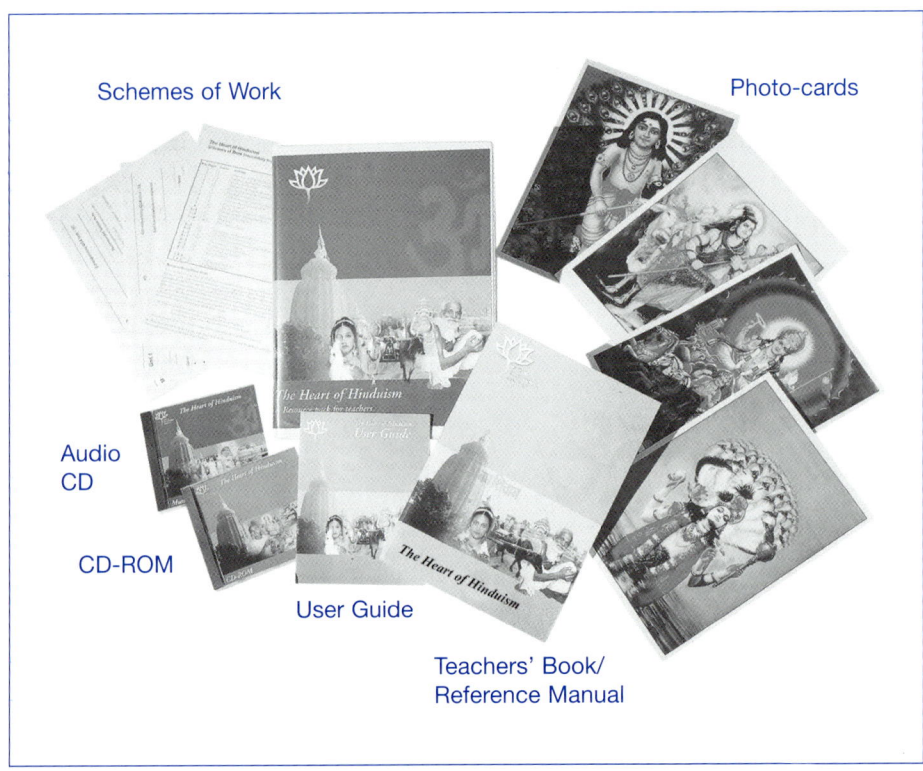

Schemes of Work

Photo-cards

Audio CD

CD-ROM

User Guide

Teachers' Book/
Reference Manual

Representing the Tradition

In writing materials on any religious tradition, there will inevitably be a degree of generalisation. Within "The Heart of Hinduism", it has been impossible to represent absolutely all Hindu perspectives. Subsequently, some Hindus will disagree with some statements in our pack – and, naturally, we respect their opinions. We are also aware that our own perspectives, from the Vaishnava tradition, may colour our presentation, though we have attempted to accurately represent all main strands, particularly those in the UK.

Faith representatives sometimes present an idealised picture of their tradition; we have tried to avoid this 'domestication', and have not shunned discussion of sensitive issues such as caste. In so doing, we have tried to promote sound methodologies along the lines of an interpretive approach, and recommend that students are encouraged to discern the many forces – material and spiritual – that shape any religious tradition. We greatly welcome a critical but empathic approach towards religion. Many of the questions included in the Teachers' Book (e.g. under 'Personal Reflection') are designed to help enhance critical thinking. Although these materials have been carefully written, the teacher should appreciate that the framework presented is limited and somewhat tentative. Be careful to avoid stereotyping and, within the constrains of funds and time, try to have contact with faith-communities. Let students hear the personal opinions of faith members, and about their own unique experiences – which may differ with those presented in this pack! A list of useful contacts is included on the CD-Rom and in the Teachers' Book.

How to Use the Pack

There is no set way of using these materials, and you can develop practices most suited to your own needs, style, etc. You may consider using the following approaches:

1. **Use the Teachers' Book** as a reader to deepen your own knowledge and understanding. Subsequently, use it to select appropriate material for classroom use. The book also contains sections to help you relate topics to AT2.

2. **Begin with the Schemes of Work** (as they correlate to your Local Agreed Syllabus and your school's own Programme of Study.)

3. **Use other materials as a 'way-in';** for example, the twelve deity photo-cards or selected audio tracks. Alternatively, you could copy selected material from the CD-Rom, including stories, articles and quotes from Hindu leaders.

Ideally, you will use all these approaches. Although, understandably, you will want to go straight to the Teaching Ideas (and other classroom resources), the pack is intended to help you become more creative and confident in developing your own learning experiences. You should also keep in mind the Teacher Support Service, which you may ring at any time – for example, if there is something you do not understand, or you require advice on writing a particular lesson plan.

Recommended and Auxiliary Materials:

We have included in this pack a select list of recommend books. In moving towards the ideal of a self-contained and comprehensive pack, we highlight two, which we have termed 'auxiliary books' and which are available from the publisher *(see page 2)*. They are as follows:

'Moral Issues in Hinduism' by Rasamandala Das (publication date, March 2004)

'Vedic Stories from Ancient India' by Ananta Shakti

All the six items included in this pack are shown on the previous page and listed on page 2. Suggestions on how to use them are given overleaf and on subsequent pages.

1 Teachers' Book / Reference Manual

This book is primarily for teachers. It is to help you better understand Hinduism, so that you can teach about it with confidence. It also contains material directly related to pupils' learning, in terms of (1) content, (2) the specific aims of RE.

You can use it many ways, most notably two:

1. **For systematic reading and study** (especially by trainees and by qualified teachers wishing to enhance their own knowledge and understanding).

2. **For reference purposes as the need arises** (for your own understanding and/or to select material suitable to student learning).

Structure of the Book

The material is laid out so that you can gain depth in any topic without wading through volumes of irrelevant text. For ease of access, it is categorised into 4 Parts and 12 Chapters, and over 100 self-contained spreads (either single or double-page). Although the design is original, it's format somewhat corresponds to the three components of Attainment Target One, 'Learning about Religion', as shown in the table below:

Part of Book	Corresponding Component of AT1
1. Concepts and Values *Chapters 1-2*	1. *Beliefs and teachings*
2. Central Practices *Chapters 3-7*	2. *Practices* & Lifestyles
3. Lifestyle and Expressions of Faith *Chapters 8-9*	2. Practices & *Lifestyles* 3. *Expression and Language*
4. Continuity and Change *Chapters 10-12*	**1, 2 & 3** *(see note 3 below)*

Please note:

1. It is impossible to categorise all religions in the same way. For example, when teaching about some religious traditions, there is need to carefully distinguish between culture and the religion itself. Within Hinduism, however, culture is an integral part of religion, an important expression of dharma. Subsequently, from a Hindu perspective, the QCA category of 'expression and language' may appear somewhat limited. Dharma is expressed through a wide range of practices. In Hinduism, therefore, language may not be as central to such expression as with those traditions that stress orthodoxy and conformity of belief.

2. Part 2 and Part 3 both explore practices, but Part 2 focuses on those that are more central to the individual's spiritual development.

3. Part 4 is consistent with an interpretive approach, recognising the fluidity of any tradition, and the dialectics between the individual, the broad tradition and the groups and sub-groups that make up that tradition. This part is important in recognising that any religion is diverse and internally contested, with tensions between the needs for both change and continuity.

Building in Attainment Target Two

One of our concerns in writing this book was to ensure that it was useful in readdressing the insufficient or superficial attention often given to Attainment Target 2, 'Learning from Religion.' There are three parts to AT2 and the book includes corresponding sections in each spread, as shown below:

Sections within the Book	Corresponding Component of AT2
'Personal Reflection'	AT2 (a) *Identity and Experience*
'Meaning and Purpose'	AT2 (b) *Meaning and Purpose*
'Related Values/Issues'	AT2 (c) *Values and Commitments*

Note; the sections called 'Personal Refection' are largely geared towards helping make the topic accessible to the teacher. You can easily adapt them for your students.

Other Features within the Book:

Key Points – main points, with which you and/or your students should be familiar. Relates to 'Knowledge'

Useful Analogies – most of these are included in Chapter One to help you come to terms with the main Hindu concepts.

Common Misunderstandings – these boxes address many of the common misunderstandings about the tradition. Relates to 'Understanding' and is also relevant to the study of different world-views, and the values and concepts underpinning them.

Related Stories – useful 'ways in'. All stories with a reference code (e.g. STO-108) are found on Tab 6 of the CD-Rom (*see page 9*).

Scriptural Passages – connected to the topic on hand. These and more are available on the CD-Rom (under Tab 7).

Quotes – by Hindu leaders and everyday people. More are available on the CD-Rom.

Photographs and Illustrations – all those in the book are available on the CD-Rom (*see page 11*).

Appendices – these include index, glossary, and lists of recommended books and useful contacts.

Note: Another feature of this book is that we have tried to be comprehensive, condensing material without omitting important facts. It represents not a random selection of information but a careful distillation. If you find important information has been inadvertently omitted, you can most likely find it on the CD-Rom (Tabs 1-5).

The CD-Rom has two main components – (1) the Interactive CD, and (2) the Print File
within Tabs 1-5, and 'resources to help teaching', mainly within Tabs 6-9. See pages

Tab 1	Tab 2	Tab 3	Tab 4	Tab 5
General Information on Hinduism	Information relating to **Part 1** of Teachers' Book	Information relating to **Part 2** of Teachers' Book	Information relating to **Part 3** of Teachers' Book	Information relating to **Part 4** of Teacher Book
	Concepts & Values	Central Practices	Lifestyles/ Expressions of faith	Continuity Change
	Chapters 1-2	**Chapters 3-7**	**Chapters 8-9**	**Chapters 10**

Notes on Tab 1–5

These 5 tabs include:

- **Fact Sheets** (written by ISKCON Educational Services)   Code: FCT
- **Articles** (various authors)   Code: ART
- **Books**   Code: BUK
- **Photo-card texts**   Code: PCT

Each item has a reference code comprising 3 letters (as shown above)
followed by the chapter number and 2 extra digits. Those starting with a zero
are general information, not specific to any chapter

e.g. ART - 001 is an **article** giving **general information**
ART - 101 is an **article** on a subject relevant to **Chapter 1**
PCT - 301 is a **photo-card text** (relevant to **Chapter 3**)
BUK - 401 is a **book** relating to **Chapter 4**
FCT - 801 is a **fact sheet** about a subject in **Chapter 8**
ART - 1001 is an **article** on a subject relevant to **Chapter 10**

All items can be viewed on screen or printed out (e.g. as student handouts)

On each, there are two main sections of content - 'further information on Hinduism', (bottom) and 16 for more details.

Tab 6	Tab 7	Tab 8	Tab 9
Stories	**Scripture & Quotes**	**Audio Glossary**	**Teaching Aids**

Notes on Tab 6

Notes on Tab 7

Notes on Tab 8 & 9
See pages 10-11

Stories

Each story has the reference code STO followed by the chapter number and 2 extra digits.

Stories are a useful way to move into a subject, especially when exploring concepts & values

By clicking on the hyperlink you will either:

1) View on screen the story, which you can also print out.

2) See a list of recommended books where the story can be found

1. **Scriptural Passages and Verses**
   a. Concepts   Code: SPC
   b. Values   Code: SPV
   c. Others   Code: SPO
   d. Verses on the Audio CD   No Code

2. **Songs and Poems**
   Songs   Code: SNG
   Poems   Code: POM

3. **Prayers and Mantras**
   Prayers   Code: PRA
   Mantras   Code: MAN

4. **Proverbs**
   Proverbs   Code: PRO

5. **Quotes**
   a. by Hindu Leaders   Code: QTL
   b. from everyday people (*not included in this edition*)

Each item has a reference code comprising 3 letters (as shown above), followed by 2 or 3 digits

These items are often useful as ways-in, and many are particularly useful in promoting an approach that acknowledges the commonality of the human experience (for example, by comparing Hindu proverbs to those with which we and students are familiar). Sections 1–3 can be used simultaneously with corresponding material on the Audio-CD *(see page 12).*

Notes on Tab 8: Audio Glossary and Pronunciation Guide

This feature is extremely useful if you are uncertain about Sanskrit and Hindi pronunciation.

- Go to Tab 8
- Find the word you require
- Click on the word – you will hear the correct pronunciation.
- The Audio Glossary is not included in this edition. The meaning of each word in the Pronunciation Guide can be found in the glossary within the Teachers' Book (pages 150-157)

Notes;

1. The pronunciation is by an Indian-speaking person, so don't worry if you can't pick up all the nuances of sound. At least you can avoid serious mistakes (e.g. by pronouncing 'Ravana' as Rar-va-na instead of the incorrect Ra-varn-a)

2. More information on Sanskriti and Hindi notation is included in the Teachers' Book, on page 2

Note on the "Search Facility" (all Tabs except 8, discussed above)

The are two facilities, on the interactive CD only, as shown below:

(1) **Word search** - featured on every screen, and is activated by clicking on the lower left-hand button named 'search'.

  (a) Simply enter one word and all items containing this word will be revealed. Click on the corresponding hyperlinks to view each item.

  (b) After checking one item, you can return to the list by clicking on the corresponding command button, entitled 'search results'.

(2) **Search by code** -

  (a) If you want to find a coded item, enter the code with no spaces (as if a single word). For example, for story 108 enter "STO-108". Make sure also that you enter the right number of digits; e.g. for Picture 60(a), enter "PIC-060(a)".

  b) On this first edition, this facility works on selected items. For other items, select them manually by going to the suitable Tab etc. (see page 16).

Note on reading and printing relevant items

(1) Most items, but not all, are available for reading and printing. The items not available for printing are the 250 Pictures and 5 of the 55 Articles.

(2) Some items in Tab 9 are not available on the Interactive CD

(3) Items can be read either on the Interactive-CD or within the Print File. The former allows easier accessibility and use for computer projection. The latter allows you to read bigger text through appropriate use of Word and, of course, both print and amend facilities. It also allow projection through Word, and you can adapt word files for other programmes, such as PowerPoint (within the terms of the copyright)

Please consult page 16 for more details.

Notes on Tab 9: Teaching Ideas

This Tab consists of three section, as shown below:

1. OHT'S (Visual Aids) – which include:

(a) **Pictures** (all photos and illustrations in the book) Code: PIC

(b) **Charts** (selected charts / other information from book) Code: CHA

The 3 letter code is followed by 3 digits, corresponding to the page in the Teachers' Book where the picture (or information in the chart) appears. Where there is more than one item per page, the code is followed by (a), (b), (c), etc. Lettering goes from top to bottom and/or in a clockwise direction.

The pictures and charts can be used:

(1) as part of a Computer Projection Presentation

(2) for printing onto Overhead Transparencies (charts only)

(3) for printing Student Handouts (charts only)

2. Teaching Tools – which include:

(a) Teaching Ideas Code: TID

(b) Teacher Guides Code: TGD

(c) Amendable Worksheets Code: WRK

(a) Teaching Ideas are learning experiences that can be built into one or more lessons. They are ideas designed to promote pedagogical creativity rather than to be merely pre-packed lessons (though rushed teachers will find that they can certainly save time). Many of these Teaching Ideas are cross-referenced from the Schemes of Work.

(b) Teacher Guides are generally useful in planning lessons, and stimulating further creativity. They also help the teacher select relevant material from Hinduism, and to identify how to integrate topics with other learning. For example, "Teacher Guide 1" can help the teacher select topics that are relevant to each of the "twelve major festivals". Some Teacher Guides are cross-referenced from both Teaching Ideas and the Schemes of Work.

(c) Amendable Worksheets are for students. They are in Microsoft Word so that teachers can amend them without having to cut and paste hardcopy. Once amended they can be stored on file, and printed as required. The teacher may also use the Charts (see above) to create further worksheets.

3. Further Resources – which include:

(a) A list of **Recommended Books**

(b) A list of **Useful Contacts**

3 Audio CD

This Audio CD can be used on a regular **CD-player** or on a **suitable computer** (with sound-card and speakers). It includes a spoken menu system, and narrative is included on most tracks. A transcript of tracks 4-10 is included in the CD-Rom (Tab 7)

There are 5 Sections and 40 tracks as shown below:

Track	Details	Track	Details
1	Introduction	21	**Section 3 Menu (Bhajan & Kirtan)**
2	Main Menu	22	The Arti Song
3	**Section 1 Menu (Scriptural Passages)**	23	Hare Krishna Mantra
4	Atman, Karma & Reincarnation	24	Sita Rama Mantra
5	Prakriti & Guna, Maya & Moksha	25	Navarati Song
6	God	26	Bhaja Hure Mana (Bengali bhajan)
7	Dharma	27	Tamil Song
8	Different Paths, Scripture and Guru	28	**Section 4 Menu (Musical Instruments)**
9	Time and Creation	29	Hand Cymbals
10	Hindu Values and Virtues	30	Tablas
11	**Section 2 Menu (Prayers & Mantras)**	31	Mridanga
12	Aum (Om)	32	Harmonium
13	The Gayatri Mantra	33	Sitar
14	Purusha Shukta Prayers (Creation)	34	Santoor
15	The 1,000 Names of Vishnu	35	Sarangi
16	Shiva Mantra	36	Shenai
17	Devi Mantra	37	Flute
18	The Pushti Marg Mantra	38	**Section 5 Menu (Background Music)**
19	Swami Narayana Mantra	39	Sounds of Vrindavana
20	Hare Krishna Mantra	40	Mayapur Shenai

The Heart of Hinduism Audio CD can be used in a number of ways. It is useful in providing an alternative to text-book learning, and for helping students appreciate something of the mood and atmosphere of Hinduism. We recommend:

(1) Using tracks in the classroom as they relate to relevant topics. These subjects include; philosophy/theology (beliefs/concepts), values, worship, prayer, meditation, mantras, music, modern Hindu groups.

(2) Using the last two tracks as background music, both in the classroom and for assemblies.

4 The Twelve Deity Photo-cards

For teachers covering Hinduism, the topic of God and the innumerable deities is often most challenging. Although Hindu doctrines vary significantly, the main schools agree on most key concepts. However, when discussing notions of the Supreme, there is considerable diversity. Furthermore, Hindu ideas are often quite different from those prevalent in the West. Therefore, we advise you to thoroughly study the topic, especially by reading pages 20-23 and 47-53 of the Teacher's Book. Do not delve deeply into this subject without first familiarising your students with preliminary concepts, such as that of the *atman*. This enables them to grasp the tradition's distinctive world-view, a necessary foundation in understanding the more complex ideas of God.

We have identified twelve main deities, of which four are most important. Quite naturally, some Hindus will disagree with this particular selection or the order in which we present them. It is not intended to be a definitive list, but simply a useful framework towards better understanding. We have therefore featured these twelve deities on the Photo-cards, with the complete list included on page 50 of the Teacher's Book. Detailed information on each deity is printed on the reverse of each Photo-card and is also available on the CD-Rom (under Tab 3, Chapter 3).

The Photo-cards are relevant to any work relating to God but the following are suggestions upon which the teacher may wish to expand:

1. Divide students into groups of three or four, and allocate a photo-card to each group. Ask students to discuss the features and symbols of each deity, and their possible significance. You might explore the attributes of God represented through the various deities (please refer to Teacher Guide 4).

2. You could ask students, again in groups, to do further research into their 'own deity' (according to set tasks/questions) and make short presentations before the class.

3. Have students identify the links between the various deities. This could be done through creative group work where each group (of say 3-4 students) is allocated one photo-card, and studies and discusses the information. Subsequently, according to set rules, groups could trade information, until they have constructed a spider-diagram showing the various connections/relationships between the twelve deities.

Note: We have recommended that the following deities should have already been studied at primary level (and these are available on Photo-cards in the primary pack):

    1 Krishna, the butter thief (accessible to very young children)
    2. Rama and Sita, and Hanuman (through the Ramayana)
    3. Lakshmi (through Diwali)
    4. Brahma, with Vishnu (through creation)
    5. Ganesh (popular with children)
    6. Shiva and Parvati (at the end of KS2)

5 Schemes of Work

There are ten units within the IES (ISKCON Educational Services) Schemes of Work, corresponding to the QCA Schemes of Work for Key Stage 3. IES units are best used in conjunction with the corresponding QCA material, though they also include suggestions for extending teaching to Key Stage 4 and Post-16. These units will also be useful if you don't wish to follow them in their entirety, but would rather select material suitable to your own Programme of Study. The ten IES units are listed below:

Unit No.	Unit Title	Corresponding QCA Unit
1	Where do we look for God? + *Hindu gods & goddesses*	7A
2	Religious Figures + *diversity of Hinduism & Hindu figures*	7A
2	Who was Lord Krishna?	7D
4	What are we doing for the environment? + *Hindu communities?*	7E
5	How do Hindu ideals affect their actions?	8C, 8D
6	What makes a Mandir special to Hindus?	8E, 8F
7	Where are we going? Hindu rites of passage	9A
8	Where does the universe come from? + *Hindu view of creation*	9B
9	Why do we suffer?	9C
10	Why are some places special to religious believers/Hindus?	9D

The section of the title in *italics* (above) indicates extension material, sections that have been added to the original QCA units (as we further discuss below). Each of the ten units consists of four pages - a 'cover page' and three 'main pages', numbered 1 to 3.

The Cover Page for each Unit

The cover page for each IES Unit differs from those on the original QCA schemes, which we recommend you to consult (and which include three important sections entitled 'About the Unit', 'Expectations' and 'Prior learning'.) The cover pages to the IES Units include an alternative three sections:

- **'General Guidelines'** provides you broad advice on delivering the relevant topic.
- **'Recommended Teacher Study'** helps you rapidly revise your own knowledge and understanding.
- **'Resources'** gives you a summary of all useful resources, most of which are included in this pack, and are listed throughout the 'main pages'. Each of these main pages is divided into three columns, as explained on the next page.

The Main Pages (numbered 1 to 3)

Column 1 – Learning Objectives

These are taken directly from the QCA Schemes of Work, though we have added numbers to each section. In some units, sections have been added to reflect the differences between Hinduism and the religions specifically covered in the QCA Units. (QCA recognises that their Schemes are only examples, and that the various religious traditions are inter-changeable to match Local Agreed Syllabuses and the religions they specify at Key Stage 3).

Column 2 – Related material / Guidelines for Teaching

This column is extremely useful in identifying sufficient material relevant to a particular topic. This is to enable you to try fresh approaches, select suitable and focused material, and move beyond 'the hackneyed' (for example, to avoid always selecting M. Gandhi when discussing Key Figures, resorting to ahimsa when exploring moral issues, and inevitably focusing on caste when examining social issues.)

This column also contains more explicit suggestions on how to teach the subject.
Arrows to the right (▶) indicate corresponding references to resources listed in column 3.

Column 3 – References / Resources

The Pack is designed to be as self-contained as possible, so that you have access to all the material required to teach a unit. Recommended resources are listed in column 3. If such material (e.g. a particular story) is not on the CD-Rom, or elsewhere in the Pack, then we have made references to 'auxiliary material' which you can purchase *(see page 5)*. You can also use the Internet/Web hyperlinks included on the CD-Rom and recommended on the cover page of each unit.

Column three also makes reference to Teaching Ideas, Teacher Guides, Worksheets, Pictures and Charts, the Audio-CD, and all the other resources within the pack.

You can access reference material and Teaching Aids on the CD-Rom by using the reference codes. You can do this manually, by knowing where to find each item *(see pages 8-11*, and the 'Quick Guide to Reference Codes' on *page 16)*. Alternatively, you can use the 'Search' facility *(see page 10)*.

Auxiliary Units

The 'contents page' (with the Schemes of Work themselves) lists further units that you might incorporate into a Programme of Study, extending up to the end of Post-16. An auxiliary pack, consisting of these or similar units, will be available from the publishers as from May 2004.

Teacher Support Services

If you have any queries about these Schemes of Work, please keep in mind our free support service, as mentioned on page 2.

Quick Guide to Reference Codes
What is on the CD-Rom and where to find it

Find the item's 3 letter "Code" in the left hand column. Look along the row to the "Tab" column to find the correct tab number. The previous two columns show you where the items appear, either in the Interactive CD, in the Print File, or in both. The column headed "No." indicates the number of items (figures may be somewhat approximate).

Code	Numerical Code	Item	No.	IC	PF	Tab
ART*	CCN + 2 digits	"Article"	55	✓	✓ ✕	1-5
BUK*	CCN + 2 digits	"Book"	5	✓	✓	1-5
FCT*	CCN + 2 digits	"Fact Sheet"	25	✓	✓	1-5
PCT*	CCN + 2 digits	"Photo-card Text"	12	✓	✓	3
STO*	CCN + 2 digits	"Story"	60	✓	✓	6
SNG	2 digits	"Songs"	4	✓	✓	7
MAN	2 digits	"Mantras"	7	✓	✓	7
POM	2 digits	"Poems"	10	✓	✓	7
PRA	2 digits	"Prayers"	25	✓	✓	7
PRO	2 digits	"Proverbs"	48	✓	✓	7
QTL	2 digits	"Quotes from Hindu Leaders"	64	✓	✓	7
SPC	3 digits	"Scriptural Passages – Concepts"	48	✓	✓	7
SPV	3 digits	"Scriptural Passages – Values"	54	✓	✓	7
SPO	3 digits	"Scriptural Passages – Others"	32	✓	✓	7
	Not coded	"Scriptural Passages on Audio CD"	39	✓	✓	7
CHA	Page of Book	"Charts"	64	✕	✓	9
PIC*	Page of Book	"Pictures"	250	✓	✕	9
TID	2 digits	"Teaching Ideas"	12	✕	✓	9
TGD	2 digits	"Teacher Guides"	12	✕	✓	9
WRK	2 digits	"Amendable Worksheets"	8	✕	✓	9
	Not coded	Further Reading (books etc.)	25+	✓	✓	9
	Not coded	Useful Contacts	20	✓	✓	9

Key and Notes:

(1) **IC** = Interactive CD. Items with a tick are included and can be viewed and projected.

(2) **PF** = Print File. Items included here can be printed, viewed and projected in Word format.

(3) **CCN** = Corresponding Chapter Number in the Teachers' Book. For example, if an article is primarily related to 'concepts', then this number = 1. If material is generic or introductory (i.e. not particularly related to any chapter) then this number = 0.

(4) In the Print File, the CCN consists of 2 digits e.g. 08 for chapter 8.

(5) Items marked with an asterisk (in the table above, next to the corresponding code) can be found using the "Search by code" facility on the Interactive CD.

(6) All but 5 Articles (ART-201, 801, 901, 1101 & 1201) are included in the Print File